schmingling™

the art of being well-connected through blatant self-promotion

Reviews and Endorsements

"Faith McKinney has done it! *Schmingling - The Art of Being Well-Connected Through Blatant Self-Promotion*, perfectly re-frames the concept of networking so that you can build meaningful, extraordinary, and very rich relationships in both your personal and professional lives. She is Indianapolis' best when it comes to networking. It is her passion. This book will help so many people who are looking to get to the next level. *Schmingling - The Art of Being Well-Connected Through Blatant Self-Promotion*, should be mandatory reading for anyone wanting to enhance their personal and professional relationships in a way that is mutually beneficial and personally rewarding. We all need to build and sustain meaningful relationships based on mutual give and take. Faith has the formula to show us how."

Jesse Brown
Dean, School of Business, Martin University, Indianapolis, IN
Author of *Investing in the Dream*, and
Pay Yourself First - The African American Guide to Wealth and Prosperity

"As I've gotten to know Faith over the years, I've realized that not only does she have a giving heart; she also cares about helping other people. She is a server and a leader. She does things with the purpose of making a difference. If ever there were somebody to learn from, listen to and enjoy, Faith is the person."

Jim Bellacera
President and Founder, *Successful Thinkers Network, Inc.*

"Faith's introduction to *Schmingling*... provides tips and strategies to increase your connections by adding a little spice to your networking – a fun read you will enjoy."

Linda Clemons
POWERED BY MOVEMENT™
Sales and Body Language Expert

schmingling™

the art of being well-connected through blatant self-promotion

faith mckinney
with Sharon Chinn

FAITH McKINNEY
Indianapolis, IN
www.faithmckinney.com

Schmingling™

By Faith McKinney with Sharon Chinn

ISBN-13: 978-1490926971
ISBN-10: 1490926976

Library of Congress Control Number: 2013917237

FAITH McKINNEY
Indianapolis, IN

www.faithmckinney.com

Copyright © 2013 by Faith McKinney with Sharon Chinn

All rights reserved. No part of this book may be reproduced without written permission from the publisher, except by a reviewer who may quote brief passages in a review; nor may any part of this book be reproduced, stored in a retrieval system or transmitted in any form or other without written permission from the publisher.

This book is manufactured in the United States of America.

Editor: Sharon Chinn,
You've Got Something To Say! Manuscript Writing and Editing Services

Proofreader: Sylvia Wilson,
SDW-Executive Virtual Assistance

Interior Design/Copy Editor/ Project Manager: Annie Gonzales,
FOR HIS GLORY Design Studio Book Designs and Promotional Materials

Cover Design: Mark Emmet Foster
Fostering Words+Images Marketing Communication Designs

DEDICATION

To my parents, Cleo and Normajo Moore:
I just want to make you proud.

This book is dedicated first to my husband, Jimmy, and my children, Donovan, Camille and Mauricia. I can never repay you for the sacrifices you've made in order for me to live my dreams. My dream is to take you around the world with access to people and places I've only dreamed about.

I also dedicate my book to Ferguson Mayfield. I prayed for a friendship like ours. You've always believed in me. You have been a true friend to me since the day we met. You know me better than I know myself. You have supported me, defended me and been there for me through it all. Thank you for allowing me to always be myself around you. Thank you for sharing my passion for *Successful Thinkers of Indianapolis*. No words can describe how much you mean to me. Our friendship is spiritual in every way. You are an amazing man and I only want for you to be happy.

And to my sister, Faith: I prayed for a relationship like ours. We grew up on the same block and were separated for decades, but we came back together as whole women. You are 100% a true friend, and I love you. Faith, you are my teacher, my sounding board, my spiritual leader and my cheerleader! I am totally myself when I am with you.

You reached out to me and have been a consistent light in my life. We are on this amazing journey together! I finally have someone with whom I can share my vision and do the work. You are a star. You are my sister in every sense of the word. Let us both surrender our success so that we will flow and our blessings will flow. No matter where you go, I will be with you. You are my rock. I thank God for you.

To my team - Sharon Chinn, Yolanda Moore, Sylvia Wilson, Annie Gonzales, Ray Embry, Mark Foster, David Bridgeforth, Linda Clemons, Rochelle Forrest, Jim Bellacera, Donna Gunselman, Sharetha Marshall, Sandra Peacock, Candi Perry, PJ Wesson, Harrison Page, Mark Hoke, Jesse Brown, *Successful Thinkers* and *Toastmasters* everywhere: I thank you, and I love you.

ACKNOWLEDGEMENTS

Stephen Covey wrote in his *Acknowledgement*:

> *"Interdependence is a higher value than independence."*

I emphatically concur! It wasn't until I came out of my shell that I began to blossom. It was my willingness to experience vulnerability and disappointment that led me to a freedom that I had only dreamed about.

With that said, I want to thank the people who allowed me to depend on them.

First, I want to thank my husband, Jimmy, for coming into my life and recognizing that I needed the freedom to express myself. You are an amazing man, and I'm so grateful for your love.

My parents, Cleotha and Normajo Moore - You gave me life, love and a fantastic foundation upon which to build my life. I am trying to live up to the good name I've been given.

All my children, Camille, Mauricia and Donovan and Lauren - You are the reason and my motivation to keep going.

To my brother, Sterling, and Anjee, my sister - Thank you for understanding (or pretending to understand) me. My niece, Simone and my nephews, Kiwane, Sterling and Kendall: I'm working to make you proud of me.

To my Aunt Rebecca - You taught me to appreciate the little things. I watched as you took care of my grandmother. I hope I'll have you around to take care of me too!

To my very best friends, Ferguson Mayfield and Faith James - What a ride we have shared! You two have been amazing to me. I prayed for the friendship we share. You are my heroes and my teachers. I love you both!

To my first mentor, Linda Clemons - I finally understand what drives you. I don't think I'll ever stop!

To my friend, Rochelle Forrest - Thank you for believing and investing in me. I won't let you down.

To Janine Yeager - Your sweet disposition and loving heart teaches me that power and strength are most potent in a small, quiet package. You amaze me!

To Dr. Eyrich - Thank you for revealing the secrets.

To Lisa Nichols - Thank you for being in "The Secret". It was important for me to see you.

To Jack Canfield - I saw you many years ago, but I didn't appreciate your gifts. Thank you for sharing your gifts with the world.

To my other mother, Ms. Dorothy McKinney - You've taught me that serving is cool! You are always giving even when you go without. You are an amazing woman who has raised an amazing man.

To Ms. Rae Harris, Ms. Anita Lee and Ms. Myra Rhodes - Thank you for taking such good care of my baby girl, Camille. I couldn't continue without your help.

To my extended family, cousins, aunts and uncles - Thank you for allowing me to be totally and completely myself, even when I wasn't quite sure who that would be. I love each and every one of you.

To my *ICIndymag* team, Mark Hoke and Harrison Page - Thank you for allowing me to grow on your dime. I couldn't have asked for a better experience.

To my *Successful Thinkers of Indianapolis* family - Thank you for allowing me to grow and stretch and have the time of my life doing it. I appreciate you!

To my coaches David Bridgeforth and Yolanda Moore - Thank you for teaching me how to express myself. I am more of myself because of you.

To Jesse Brown - Thank you for your guidance and friendship.

To Marc Allen and *Butler University* - Thank you for bringing such great individuals to my community.

To Matthew Steward - Your vision and kindness are remarkable. You certainly are a gift to me. Thank you for allowing me to live my dreams.

To *Toastmasters International* - Thank you for providing a platform for me to practice my craft. I am growing by leaps and bounds.

To Jim Bellacera - Thank you for your vision and persistence. I would never have had this wonderful life if you hadn't followed your dreams.

To Terence R. Winslow - Thank you for teaching me about what leaders do. You are truly a man of integrity. It was destiny and fate that we met. I will write about it more formally. I wouldn't have believed it if I hadn't been there.

To Caroline Robbins - Thank you for your persistence about *Send Out Cards*. My life is much richer because of you and *Send Out Cards*.

To Jason Miller - Thank you for challenging me to push my boundaries.

To George Benson, Hill Harper, Shirley Murdock, Dan Rather, Soledad O'Brien, Freda Payne, Tavis Smiley, and Kirk Franklin - Thank you all for allowing me to practice my interviews with you.

To George Fraser - Thank you for sharing your wisdom and your catfish dinner with me!

To Dr. Herbert Harris - Thank you for sharing your friendship and wisdom with me. I'll always remember your kindness.

To Oprah Winfrey - Thank you for being the greatest example of how I will live my life. Thank you for continuing to provide thoughtful and uplifting content for to help me to learn and grow.

To my co-workers at Eastgate Post Office - Thank you all for allowing me the flexibility to live my dreams.

To my *Facebook* family - You are the best!!!!

Thank You God for guiding me through this part of my journey.

FAITH McKINNEY

FOREWORD

When I first met Faith, she was all over the place - but in a good way. She was attending every event under the sun with no clear purpose other than to meet as many people as she possibly could. She was considering various network marketing ventures, and she didn't mind working with anyone. The one thing that was clear was Faith knew she had a message that she wanted to share with the world.

Building quality, lasting relationships is one of the keys to sustained success. Faith has been able to do that by applying her own system of networking that she dubbed "*Schmingling*," and through her system, she has tapped into various markets that she once only dreamed of. She has been able to meet people in the industry that she had only known through their books and audio CDs.

Through careful strategy and consistent brand building, Faith McKinney has literally become "The Great Connector," helping people achieve their dreams by building meaningful relationships. Forget everything you thought you knew about networking, and read this book with an open mind so that you too can expand your network. Follow the steps outlined in this book, and let Faith McKinney connect you to your destiny. You will be glad you did.

Yolanda Moore
2X *WNBA Champion*, Brand Consultant,
and Author of *You Will Win If You Don't Quit*

CONTENTS

INTRODUCTION

Chapter 1	Does Everybody Really Know Your Name?	1
Chapter 2	Schmingling Makes You Attractive – It's All Energy!	7
Chapter 3	How to Be In the Right Place At the Right Time	11
Chapter 4	Your Media Kit: Tell the World Who You Are	13
Chapter 5	Interning: How to Get a Free Education	15
Chapter 6	What's Your Motivation?	17
Chapter 7	Introvert or Extrovert? That Is the Question!	21
Chapter 8	If You Are Not Online You Are Invisible	23
Chapter 9	Power Schmingling – It's Not for the Faint of Heart	25
	Schmingling Photo Gallery	27
Chapter 10	Pretend that Everybody Loves You	31
Chapter 11	Don't Break Character	37
Chapter 12	Understand the Jargon of Your Industry	43
Chapter 13	Don't Be a Schmuck – Look the Part	47
Chapter 14	Gifts that Keep On Giving – Offering Access	53
Chapter 15	How to Prove You Are an Expert in Your Field	57
Chapter 16	Make Others Want to Connect With You	59
Chapter 17	Schmingling Won't Work if You Don't Have This	61
Chapter 18	The Schmingler's Way to Enter a Room	65
Chapter 19	7 Rules for Schmingling Engagement	67
Chapter 20	My Guaranteed, No Fail, Best Schmingling Tactic You Must Do Today!!!	69
	Frequently Asked Schmingling Questions	71
	About the Author, **Faith McKinney**	76
	Team Schmingling Bios	78

INTRODUCTION

"*Schmingling...*" It's an unlikely title for a book about connecting and blatant self-promotion, but I like to use this analogy because as an introvert, I needed to find a way to overcome my shyness and fear of connecting with people while putting myself out there to publicize my skills.

Schmingling is a term I use to describe a combination of schmoozing and mingling. To schmooze is defined as being ingratiating towards somebody. Mingle means: To circulate among a group of people, such as guests at a party, according to *Encarta Dictionary*.

I combined the two terms to define *Schmingling* as the art of being well-connected through blatant self-promotion, which, consequently, is the book's title.

Ever since I was in preschool, I wanted to be popular, outgoing and fun! I noticed how my best friend, Shannon Brown, was always at ease around teachers and students alike. Her effervescent personality and infectious smile made her as popular with teachers as she was with students. She always seemed to know exactly what to say and do.

As I moved on to grade and middle school, I noticed the same phenomena with different people. I was in a bigger school with even more boys and girls who seemed to be bigger than life! They appeared to be more fun, smarter, and a lot more interesting than I was. I craved the attention they received from other students as well as teachers. While I was trapped in what seemed to be a voiceless body crying to get out, the popular kids enjoyed life and all it had to offer, or so it seemed to me at the time.

I knew that I wanted to be one of those popular kids who always knew what to say and when to say it. I wanted people to laugh at my jokes no matter how lame they were, and I wanted to be the center of attention. My mission, then, was to know at least one person everywhere I went. That meant I needed to be on a first name basis with a lot of people! My goal was to receive a warm welcome even in the most foreign places. Most importantly, I wanted to be recognized for my kindness and stellar reputation, which meant that I needed to stay away from trouble at any cost.

In short, I wanted to be a star!

When I realized that *Schmingling* was the way to achieve these goals, I was excited to know that there were techniques and skills I could learn. The only question I asked myself was, "How can I help others with this information?" Well, this book, *Schmingling - The Art of Being Well-Connected Through Blatant Self-Promotion*, is the answer. In this book, I will show you the same methods I use to make a name for myself and expand my opportunities every day of my life. It's not a guide to acting like someone you're not. Instead, it guides you to be more of the person you really are: a "Great Connector"!

You'll discover the 5 C's of *Schmingling* explained within this book.

1. CREATIVITY - Create the life you imagine.
2. CONFIDENCE - Plan, prepare and believe that you are worthy.
3. CREDIBILITY - Command more money; gain respect in your industry; and access to more people and opportunities.
4. CONSISTENCY - Be authentic in your life at all times. Keep it REAL.
5. CONNECTIVITY - Maintain the relationships you want in your life by staying connected through *Schmingling*!

I have explained them here so that as you read you will be conscious of the elements of the 5 C's throughout this book. So let's get started!

My hope for you is that by studying this book, your mind is opened to the infinite possibilities of *Schmingling* and that you will transcend any boundaries you have consciously or unconsciously erected for yourself in order for you to be positioned to succeed beyond your wildest dreams!

Yours,
FAITH McKINNEY

chapter 1

Does Everybody Really Know Your Name?

Schmingling is like most fan-based building activities in that you do it consistently and with an end in mind. Whether your goal is to retire comfortably, to get votes on a television talent show, or to grow your business into a world-class organization, you always start with the end in mind.

Define your ultimate destination and understand what it looks like when you've achieved it. Your focus must be clear and specific enough that you can state it in one sentence. Think of it this way: Your goal is your mission stated clearly in its essence in a single sentence. A strong dose of self-confidence will help you get there!

The important point here is to be crystal clear about your end goal.

Maya Angelou said,

> "Clarity is more than a concept; it's a way of life."

Does your face light up when you think about your goal? When you are clear about what you want, you attract people and situations that you desire because you are focused on that desire. These people are your fans!

Schmingling means having clarity about yourself and what you do, thereby, making it easy for your fan base to spread the word and build your reputation.

How to Define Your Target Niche

Webster's Dictionary defines a brand as: *"A particular product that is produced or distributed by a company, distinguished from products offered by competing companies by a name, symbol or design."* When you think of the lead character in the play, *Annie*, you understand the character's brand. *Annie* is bubbly, precocious, loving, and full of energy and loves her little dog, Sandy. *Annie*'s brand is her bright red dress, black shoes, black belt, white collar and white socks, her curly red hair, freckles, vivacious, precocious personality and infectious smile.

This is *Little Orphan Annie*'s brand. You have a brand as well. Are you known for bringing delicious baked goods to the office? Are you on every bowling league in your city? Are you an accounting genius? Do you have a fabulous smile? Do you support causes for women? Are you always the biggest donor to charities? If you are known for something, that is your brand. This is how others see you and describe you, whether you know it or not. It's as simple as that. Defining your brand is challenging because the way you see yourself may be different from the way others see you.

Ask a few trusted friends or family members to describe you. Allow them to be honest without interrupting them. Ask them what they feel you are good at. Listen intently as they give you nuggets of information about whom they feel you are. They are offering you a huge gift!

Many traits may be repeated by different family members or friends, which means that these particular attributes are very dominant. Do this with as many friends and family as you can. Consider the most repeated trait(s) as being your signature niche. You may not totally agree with the results of your informal survey, but there is probably truth to the feedback you are receiving.

If your results contain traits that you do not wish to perpetuate, there is hope! By creating a link between the popular trait result and what you'd like to be known for, then you can more easily discover a niche for yourself, as well as work on discarding those traits by which you do not want to be identified.

Chapter 1   Does Everybody Really Know Your Name?

So What? You're No Saint!

Having a good reputation and being seen as a leader and expert does not require that you be a saint, however. Just look at shock jock, Howard Stern.

For years he's worked as a radio disc jockey that was known for being outrageous, opinionated, rude, arrogant, vile and downright obnoxious. His show was incredibly popular, and they even aired the radio show on television, further perpetuating the Howard Stern brand of entertainment to a broader audience.

The question becomes, *"Why is Howard Stern so popular?"* The answer is that he is consistently Howard Stern. He has a reputation that his fan base is attracted to. He has integrity which only means that he stands doggedly by his beliefs without wavering. His fan base trusts Howard to be quintessentially himself.

Don't Avoid the Obvious

I took this survey, myself, many years ago when I began my speaking career. Since my daughter, Camille, is a special needs child, many of my professional speaking mentors told me to speak about Camille. They told me that by speaking about being the parent of a child with special needs, I would have an audience of millions and make a huge difference in the world. Unfortunately I didn't agree with these professionals. Because I was in denial about having a child with special needs, I never wanted to appear as a victim. I felt that going around the world speaking on *"woe is me"*, *"poor me"* and *"life is so hard"* topics that I would succumb to being a victim. I never wanted to be viewed as a victim, and speaking about my daughter seemed to do just that.

Instead, I wanted to be known for my contributions to the world. I wanted to speak and write about how I succeeded in the business world and earned millions of dollars by helping people. I denied my own obvious niche, even up to the time of this writing. I'm sad about feeling this way about speaking about my own child. I just hope that revealing the feelings I have will help someone who may feel the same way. Email me to let me know if this message speaks to your heart.

It wasn't until a conversation I had with John Girton, a young, dynamic pastor in Indianapolis, who is also a professional speaker and my marketing mentor, that I finally saw the light. Until that conversation, I could never understand why I had so much difficulty earning a living as a speaker on the topic of business. For years, I wallowed in near poverty as I helped others *Schmingle* and create wealth. Why wasn't the same advice I was giving others working for me financially?

Pastor G reminded me that I am an expert at being a mother and raising a special needs child to adulthood. He revealed to me that my experiences, challenges, highs and lows could spread healing throughout the world. He taught me that my story, and how I tell it, would become my legacy. He also shared with me how I could speak about Camille without perpetuating a victim mentality by using certain speaking techniques. After learning this, I began to open myself up to the possibility of changing the world with Camille's story.

Accentuate Your Positives and the Weaknesses

As an introvert, I realized that in order to be more confident and comfortable in front of people, I needed to put myself in a position to be vulnerable. I began studying with David Bridgeforth, a protégé of the world famous motivational speaker, Les Brown. I also needed to do something that would push me beyond my comfort zone.

I was never attracted to acting. I think it's because I couldn't understand why anyone would voluntarily memorize lines, get up in front of an audience, and talk! Acting was not on my radar, but as it turns out, it was exactly what I needed.

My cousin, Adrienne Peck, first suggested that I audition for a local play that she had seen advertised. The stage play was called *Living Fat*. When Adrienne mentioned acting, I immediately began to resist, internally, just as I had resisted speaking about my daughter. Then I thought to myself that since I was only acting, and it was not who I really was, the idea of acting didn't seem so formidable. I must say that acting on stage is much more involved and difficult than I ever imagined. Even so, I garnered one of the

Chapter 1   Does Everybody Really Know Your Name?   5

lead roles, even though it was my very first time acting. I had no idea what I was doing, but I did want this play to be a success. Many people had put in many hours of work even before my audition. I quickly learned that acting is not a solo sport.

Other actors, the director, stagehands, grips, journalists and our audience had all invested time and energy into this project. Therefore I wanted my performance to be perfect. So from the moment I got the part, to the final bow, I was thoroughly and completely engaged in this play. I studied my lines and rehearsed every single day for one month. I studied other actors and learned their lines too. And when it was time to perform...I forgot my lines! Ugh!!! There is nothing more embarrassing or humbling than forgetting your lines in front of an audience.

Then I went on to star in the first online soap opera with an all-African-American cast, filmed entirely in Indianapolis, Indiana. I caught the acting bug! During filming, I continued working full-time while taking care of my family. The time and financial constraints of the cast and crew made it impossible to complete the series in a reasonable amount of time. It took four months to complete twenty-one, three to five minute episodes, and another three months to complete editing and get it online. You can still see it at: *www.Confessions55.com*. It's for this reason that I now prefer film acting over stage acting. Film has its advantages. In film, you don't necessarily have to learn the entire movie script to excel. Film can be edited, and lines can be fed to you in case you forget. Since film is a lot more forgiving than stage, I prefer film over stage acting. With film, you can also sometimes work around schedules and correct errors before anyone sees them. The upside to stage acting is instant gratification. You can hear the cheers and applause immediately. The sense of accomplishment is much greater on stage, but since my schedule is so tight, I tend to forget my lines, no matter how much I study. That's why I'll stick to film.

Always Be Yourself

Understanding what works for you can save you a lot of headaches. Many times, in an effort to impress others, we may stretch ourselves much too far affecting our results negatively. Though biting off more than you can chew can, on the surface, appears to be a bad idea, consider biting off more than you can chew, and keep chewing! It's true that it's not fair to deliver inferior quality when others are depending on you to deliver the best, and you do need to understand what you are well suited to do; however, don't refuse challenges just because they may not play to your strengths. Find what works for you, but also allow yourself to be stretched and adapt your solutions, using those strengths in areas outside your comfort zone.

Chapter 2

Schmingling Makes You Attractive – It's All Energy!

Your energy level is attractive to others with your matching energy level.

Have you ever walked into a meeting with a room full of people who looked as if they had all lost their best friend? No one is saying a word, but judging by the feeling you got as soon as you crossed the threshold, you felt heavy and tired. The energy in the room was that low.

Talk show queen, Oprah Winfrey, says,

> *"You are responsible for the energy you bring."*

What does that mean? I'm glad you asked. Think about the room I mentioned earlier. Imagine yourself in the room along with the other low energy people. You begin to feel depressed and drained of energy just like the others in the room. Your contribution to the energy was energy that resonated with the energy that was already in the room, therefore you continued the cycle of low energy.

Becoming responsible for your energy takes some forethought and a little courage. Prior to entering the room, imagine everyone is happy to see you. Imagine yourself as the Belle or Beau of the Ball! Stand as if you won the *Academy Award* for Best Actor. Own the imaginary room!

I had experienced this phenomenon recently at the mall with my kids. I am currently experiencing a horrendous case of adult acne. I haven't had a breakout this bad in almost ten years. Let me tell you, I truly understand how it feels when you don't feel that you look your best because of circumstances beyond your control. For years I suffered from poor self-esteem and low self-image mainly due to acne blemishes. Acne and the resulting blemishes can make the most outgoing person feel like hiding. And that's what I did. I wore sunglasses consciously hoping no one would speak to me because I looked so different from my media photos.

I even said to my son, "*I feel like an old mother.*" I felt the old me resurfacing. I noticed even salespeople didn't approach me as they usually did. I felt invisible. My normally vivacious personality was buried beneath layers of shame, embarrassment and low self- esteem. I went to purchase acne medicated products from a kiosk in the mall, and I mentioned to the saleslady that I felt that my self-esteem was very low. As I heard myself say this, I knew it was time to put my teachings into practice for myself. Immediately I remembered how confident and beautiful I felt when my face was clear. I put a smile on my face as I usually do wherever I go. I stood up straight; I lifted my sunglasses so my eyes were visible. I filled my lungs with nice deep breaths of air, and I began to feel happy. I gave good eye contact to everyone. I freely gave compliments to strangers. I laughed with salespeople, and interacted with others. I was my gorgeous self again! I held my head high as I continued my shopping at the mall.

Within ten minutes, two very handsome men began conversations with me. I even got a business card! I felt like myself again, even though the condition of my face remained unchanged. What did change were both my focus and my energy level.

Energy is everything, and everything is energy!

What you focus your energy or your attention on grows. Try this experiment: The next time you are feeling self-conscious for any reason, imagine yourself when you are at your best. This is your most powerful self. That could be when you are creating a beautiful masterpiece in your studio, in the gym working up a sweat, or closing an important deal at the office.

Remember that feeling, and really feel the feeling in your heart. Feel it until you smile in your bones! Feel your posture improve. Notice your breathing

Chapter 2 Schmingling Makes You Attractive – It's All Energy!

get deeper with more air filling your lungs. As you concentrate on this feeling, begin your activity with this new energy at work. Try this exercise prior to your next networking event. When you exit your vehicle in the lot of the venue, remember to do this exercise:

- Concentrate on your most powerful self - *the self you are when you are at your best.*
- Feel the feeling of true happiness and control.
- Fill your lungs with air.
- Lift your head up high!
- Take longer strides and make no apologies!

As you do this, notice how others respond to you while you are in this high state of energy. As you enter the venue, take note of the energy you feel in the room. You can tell if you feel like the room is "dead" or "lively and fun".

- Are people interacting with each other?
- Is there a lot of activity, or are people sitting quietly speaking to each other?
- Are there familiar faces in the room?
- How is the lighting? Is it dim or bright?
- Is the room sunlit or are fluorescent bulbs the source?
- Is there music in the background? Is it loud or soft?
- Is the room crowded or relatively empty?

All of these conditions affect the energy of a room. Nevertheless, you are responsible for the energy you bring to the room. This is great news because no matter what external conditions exist, you control the energy you attract internally by doing the exercise I described above. Your energy level is attractive to others who possess the same energy level, so it is critical to raise your energy level whenever you are feeling a little down.

Chapter 3

How to Be In the Right Place At the Right Time

One of the objectives of the art of *Schmingling* is to meet someone who may connect you to someone who could potentially help to get you where you want to be.

Being in the right place at the right time is more than luck. It's paying attention to the business, social and civic calendars of major organizations around you. It doesn't matter if you live in New York, L.A. or Indianapolis; you can meet people who control purse strings and boardrooms in any city.

It is vitally important to be properly packaged before approaching your person of influence. An established brand, a proven track record, testimonials, plus photos or a video are composites of the resume you'll need to capture the attention of your influencer. Always provide proof of your claim with this content on your website or in your professionally prepared media kit. Sounds like a tall order? Yes, it is, but with time and planning, you can increase your visibility and win the favor of the people who can drive your success.

Effective *Schmingling* means doing some research about the values and hobbies of your intended influencer or audience. All true leaders have a cause or project that is near and dear to their hearts. It is your job to find out where your influencer's heart lies. With the help of the Internet, it is relatively easy to gather this information. Upon discovering the boards that your influencer serves on, or what cause they champion, you should then go and volunteer to work for the causes they support. Attend charity events, be a large contributor, or simply send them a card with a photo of you volunteering.

I did this once with remarkable results. I enjoy researching local and industry leaders through trade journals and publications of schools or organizations. A few years ago, I read the Alumni magazine of the *Indiana University Maurer School of Law* in Bloomington, Indiana. I came across an article written about Attorney James. Jim is the high profile, criminal defense attorney who first represented boxer Mike Tyson following his arrest in Indianapolis back in 1991.

As I read the article, I noted how Jim appeared to be a person who truly loved his career and was extremely happy with his life. Learning more about him, I was compelled to make contact to let him know how much I enjoyed the article and why I admired him as a person. I handwrote a note on one of those free note cards you get when charities are soliciting donations. One thing I did do to make my note stand out was to write the address in calligraphy. I also put my phone number at the end of my note. I mailed it, not really expecting a response; but nearly a week later, it happened! I received a call from Jim Voyles himself! He was extremely impressed by my note and wanted to meet me in his downtown Indianapolis office ASAP!

When I arrived at Jim's office, he greeted me as if I were royalty! This was a surreal experience. I had no idea what to say, so I decided that I should just be myself. I asked him questions about his life, his family and his hobbies. I found out where he went to high school, the names of his children, and his passion for Indy car racing! At the end of our meeting, I asked to take a picture with him. This is a very important step! I'll explain in a later section, but suffice it to say, I now send Jim Voyles a card at least once per year with our picture in it. I don't think he'll ever forget me!

This is what I learned from writing: I learned that many people don't take time to handwrite letters. I also learned that seemingly small gestures really do mean a lot.

Being at the right place at the right time can be done literally anywhere, but just remember to be yourself when you do meet your influencer.

Chapter 4

Your Media Kit: Tell the World Who You Are

Marketing yourself in the *Schmingling* arena requires a media kit.

With the explosion of social networking sites online, marketing yourself is no longer a luxury reserved for only C-level job seekers. Tooting your own horn is MANDATORY!!!

> *"Do what others aren't willing, crazy or savvy enough to do."*
> ~ David Seaman

There are literally millions of people all over the world vying for the attention of employers and people of influence. When you are competing for a position, having an edge could make or break the deal. Why not give yourself the advantage with a professionally produced marketing kit? A marketing kit consists of the following: a current, professional photo, a bio, a vision statement, a mission statement, letters of recommendation, articles you've written, articles written about you, photos, videos and more, all placed prominently online on your website or on your social networking sites, such as *Facebook*.

Let me say this now, even though I think it should be a given: if you don't have a website or *Twitter* or *Facebook* page, you are not even in the game! Stop what you are doing right now and create a *Facebook* page!!!

There, my rant is over!

Earlier this year I hired Yolanda Moore, a branding and life coach and two-time *WNBA Champion* for the *Houston Comets*, to guide me in creating my media kit. I say Yolanda guided me in creating my media kit because she did not do it for me; she kept me focused to create it for myself.

She helped me with:

- Brand Development
- Bio
- Speaker Introduction
- Cover Letters
- Blog
- Copywriting
- Featured Articles

Having a crisp, clean, up-to-date media kit will give your intended audience, influencers and media a look into your body of work that is flattering to you. Understanding the importance of a good, current media kit could mean commanding and receiving fees that pay up to ten times more than being without a winning media kit. Think of your media kit as a movie trailer you see prior to seeing the feature film. If the movie trailer is exciting to look at, you'll probably want to see more about that particular film. If the trailer is lackluster, I guarantee that you will not be investing an evening watching that movie.

Take the time and make the investment on a stellar media kit, and put it online!

Chapter 5

Interning: How to Get a Free Education

I have a confession: I never graduated from college.

There! I said it! It's always been a small bone of contention with my parents, however, I now long for those college experiences like parties, pledging and interning. I never interned until I was well into adulthood. In fact, I interned for my first speaking coach, David Bridgeforth, who is now a magazine publisher of his own *DBQ Magazine* and protégé of the world famous motivational speaker, Les Brown. As David's intern, humility was one of the most important lessons I learned during my two years of coaching.

I must also preface this by saying that I attended high school and graduated with David's parents. Although David is just three days older than my daughter Camille, while I was interning, I gave David the respect he deserved as my coach. I was honored to be able to work with such a gifted young man.

There were many times when, as an intern, I ran errands, made trips to the airport, held bags, and most of all, learned to hold my tongue. Learning when to listen is the most important element of speaking. This was just one of the nuggets I gleaned from David, not to mention the times I was able to meet really great people such as Les Brown.

I remember David calling me early one morning asking if I could pick up Les Brown at the airport within a few hours. I was at work at the time, but

I knew this was a chance of a lifetime for me. I was more than excited; I was ecstatic but also somewhat embarrassed about the 2007 gray *Ford* minivan I was driving. I would have loved to have been able to impress Les Brown in a beautiful, quiet, luxury car. Instead, I picked him up in my "Mom Van", complete with popcorn and French fries in the seats, and my paperwork on the floor. I left work, drove downtown to pick up David, and then on to the airport to pick up Mr. Brown. As Les entered my van, he greeted me warmly, but my first reaction in my mind was to apologize for the condition of his ride. However, I didn't apologize. I held my tongue. It was what it was, dirt and all! Les Brown asked if I knew where he could get a haircut and a razor shave. "*Yes!*" I replied, and I quickly called my uncle who owns a very popular old-school barbershop. I told my uncle that Les Brown was coming, and please have a chair open.

On the way from the airport, I missed my turn, so getting to the barbershop took much longer than it should have. But on the way, Les had a conference call to make. He was on the phone with board members of a corporation who were deciding whether or not to have Les Brown speak at their corporate event. I got a chance to hear Les Brown at work, the real work of convincing board members that he is worth every penny of his speaking fee. It was humbling and a little uncomfortable to witness the great Les Brown on a human level. No matter how big or well known you are, selling yourself and your brand is never ending. As Les Brown says, "*Success is never ending.*"

Consistency is the secret of high achievers. It's time to break new records... set a new standard...and surpass your personal best. Look life in the eye and say, "*Bring it on!*" You were born to win. Reach down deep within, and unleash your power and your GREATNESS!

It was good to know that Les Brown practices what he preaches! Listening in on that conversation, as I drove Les Brown and David, I learned a lot that day, and I realized how fortunate I was to be able to witness the real work that this giant in the speaking industry has to maintain, even though he is at the top of his field. The lesson for me was this: The opportunity offered to interns is a gift, wrapped up to look like slavery!

Chapter 6

What's Your Motivation?

Why do you do what you do? More times than not, people do things and repeat patterns of behavior unconsciously. Some people follow in the footsteps of their parents because it's easier than figuring out life's possibilities on their own, or because the family business may present an easier path to them than pursuing something else. Others are in survival mode, taking unfulfilling jobs because it pays the bills and keeps a roof over their heads and food on the table. Still others do only what is expected of them, regardless of the degree of personal satisfaction gained or not gained from their occupation or lifestyle.

Whenever an actor studies a role, he or she always considers the motivation of the character. Even if the character they are considering is a rock.

Motivation is the engine that moves energy.

In acting, this means that you put yourself in the character's shoes. You actually embody the character not just physically, but psychologically and emotionally, as well. An actor must inhabit the character in order to determine why the character behaves as he or she does. Motivation will ultimately determine how we, the audience, view the character on stage or screen. Even if the actor is playing a simple rock, the character of the rock and its origin must be examined thoroughly in order for the actor to fully understand the rock.

This is also true for *Schmingling*. Self-examination is required to fully understand why you behave as you do and what rewards you gain by your actions or behaviors. Why do you live where you live? Why do you do the work you do? Do you enjoy your life? What are your dreams and goals? Are you living the life you truly want to live? If so, why? If not, why not?

Your motivation could have been sparked in you at a very young age.

I have a young cousin named Reilin who grew up in a very dysfunctional home. His father was out of work, addicted to drugs and paralyzed by a gunshot wound after a bad drug deal. His older brother spent years in prison, and his sister was shot in the head by her abusive boyfriend in front of her children, including her toddler daughter and infant son. In spite of this young man's seemingly tragic life, Reilin is in medical school studying to be a neurosurgeon! How is it that despite his less than ideal environment and the lack of role models in his home, he still had the incredible desire to fulfill his nearly insurmountable dream of becoming a neurosurgeon?

Years ago, when Reilin and I were at the bedside of his sister, who was in the hospital only hours before she succumbed to the gunshot wound to the head, I watched in awe as Reilin lovingly held his sister's hand and wiped the moisture off of her face as she lay dying. I felt honored to bear witness to such a profound gesture of love Reilin had for his sister. The room was silent and heavy with emotion, and I could only hope and pray that Reilin's sister would recover and resume her role of mother to two very young children.

Needing to break the deafening silence, and wanting to satisfy my curiosity, I asked Reilin what motivated him to become a brain surgeon. Immediately his eyes brightened, and the weight of the room lifted. His reply was something I never expected. Reilin replied that it was a grade school field trip that motivated him to want to become a doctor. He stated that on one particular trip, his class was shown a human brain in a jar. Apparently this brain in a jar was just enough to move this young man through monumental life, academic and financial challenges.

Whatever motivates you is extremely personal and unique to you. However, just like Reilin, the mere mention of your motivation should make your eyes light up and your heart sing.

I don't know about you, but my dream has always been to be rich, famous

Chapter 6   What's Your Motivation?

and to help a lot of people. This dream was personified for me when my dad took me to Amway rallies when I was thirteen years old. The Amway Corporation has a great reputation for fostering leaders and entrepreneurs. At the rallies, the top performers in the organization would be lined up on stage, dressed in the most beautiful gowns and tuxes I'd ever seen. Then each of the leaders with their spouses would step up to the microphone and tell their rags-to-riches stories of how they persisted, beat incredible odds, and succeeded. Many of the stories were so touching that I remember them to this day!

One story was told by a woman who had helped her husband build their business from lower middle class to multi-millionaire status. She mentioned the plight of one of her close friend's husband who was dying, and the family could not afford to pay for his funeral. The woman went on to say how grateful she was to have a business that provided a lifestyle that she could help people in their time of need. She then said something that I'll never forget. She said: "*You can do more to help with cash than a casserole.*" I want to be like this woman. I want to help others. For this reason, I feel it is my mission to realize my dream of fame. I continue to envision myself standing onstage in a beautiful gown, telling my rags-to-riches story.

Chapter 7

Introvert or Extrovert? That Is the Question!

Do you get excited by being among lots of people? Does an intimate gathering float your boat, or would you rather be alone most of the time? There is no right or wrong answer, but there is definitely an answer.

Understanding your tolerance for others is important to determine your optimal *Schmingling* environment. *Schmingling* requires a degree of comfort and relaxation in order for you to appear confident and capable to others. If you know that crowds and parties are not your thing, do your best to avoid *Schmingling* events that are too far removed from your comfort level. I don't mean avoid all *Schmingling* events, and I certainly don't mean avoiding the once-a-year company event where you know your influencers will be.

Your *Schmingling* style can be accommodated by various creative methods, from crowded sporting events and company parties to the more subdued book discussions or dining outings among acquaintances. Determining your style and tolerance level will allow you to be in control of your *Schmingling* arena.

I host a free monthly *Schmingling* event called *Successful Thinkers of Indianapolis*. Our events cater to adults, ages 30 to 65, generally college-educated, middle class people who work full time and own start up businesses. Attendance at our events ranges between 25 and 60 people, on average, depending on the theme of the month. Wine tastings tend to draw a larger crowd.

Successful Thinkers of Indianapolis tries to add value to *Schmingling* by:

- Offering a very personal greeting and name tag, hand-written in calligraphy
- Providing quality speakers, including local business and community leaders, major sports champions, White House advisors and authors
- Providing a very relaxed, upscale environment
- Free admission
- Providing a platform for entrepreneurs to build their credibility
- Encouraging a strong social media presence
- Providing volunteer opportunities

Chapter 8

If You Are Not Online You Are Invisible

As I mentioned earlier, you **need** an online presence. Period!

Many of the aforementioned attributes about *Successful Thinkers of Indianapolis* are not unique to *Successful Thinkers of Indianapolis*. Despite our many advantages, some aspects of our *Schmingling* style are not agreeable to everyone.

Creating your own platform for *Schmingling* is highly encouraged. Even if you are an introvert, there are ways to *Schmingling* successfully without talking to a soul.

My definition of fame is: high visibility, name recognition, integrity, a strong brand and a stellar reputation. Everything I do now leads me to that goal, and I am closer now more than ever. In order to achieve my goal of fame, I had to adapt my networking style and methods to achieve maximum visibility and brand, or name recognition branding. Increasing visibility is a relatively simple process, although it takes time and energy to generate a strong brand and name recognition.

Social media such as *Facebook*, *YouTube*, *Twitter*, *Instagram*, and many more, make being visible easier than ever! For years I have tried to get our local news to do a story about me in my effort to be on television. I would send press releases, email to newsrooms and producers, write articles, etc., with no results. I then began to think about ways to tell my own story to a large number of people in the way I want to tell it.

Social media was my answer. It's no surprise that thousands of people have been discovered on social media. Maintaining a presence on social media will increase your visibility when you understand its matrix. On *Facebook* alone, you could potentially be seen by 100,000 people and more each time you post online. Creating videos and posting them to YouTube, a video sharing website, is another powerful method for gaining visibility online. I had a professionally produced, promotional video created just for me! The video contains footage that displays to the audience my personality, range and experience in a sixty-second sound bite.

Another great thing about this promotional video is that I can repost it at any time, especially when I don't have new content to post online. This is a major benefit because there are always people who love to revisit my older posts and videos. It's like having your own television studio where you control the show and show times!

Blog, Blog, Blog!

What is a blog? According to *Wikipedia*: A **blog** (a contraction of the words **web log**)[1] is a discussion or informational site published on the *World Wide Web* and consisting of discrete entries ("posts") typically displayed in reverse chronological order (the most recent post appears first). Until 2009 blogs were usually the work of a single individual, occasionally of a small group, and often covered a single subject. More recently multi-author blogs (MABs) have developed, with posts written by large numbers of authors and professionally edited. Blog can also be used as a verb, meaning *to maintain or add content to a blog*.

Blogging is a Godsend for introverts! Credibility and expert status begins with an informed point of view. Blogging about your niche or even blogging about an opinion can help solidify your expert status. Although blogging by itself may not get you into the expert space, you can consolidate your best posts into a published book or *eBook*. Then, your expert status is one step closer.

Chapter 9

Power Schmingling – It's Not for the Faint of Heart

One of the best *Schmingling* tips I've ever received was from a book called *It* by Paula Froelich, a *Page 6* gossip reporter for *The New York Post*. In *It,* Paula lists several practical tactics many people have used to get the attention of influencers, publicists and talent agents.

The Bald, Black Belly Dancer!

Years ago, a very popular game show came to Indianapolis to search for potential contestants. The audition was sponsored by one of the local television stations, which advertised the audition for weeks. The audition was the talk of the town, and I knew this was my chance to finally get on television. As Paula Froelich instructed, I did my research. I knew that one particular television station would cover the audition, so all I needed to do was find out which reporter would cover it.

I knew that one reporter covers the station's local fluff stories, the stories that weren't so serious or controversial. I looked up the reporter's bio and email address. I then had to create a story for her to cover. I asked if she would be interested in interviewing a "Bald, Black Belly Dancer." I would even teach her a few moves. She said yes!!! She agreed to meet me at a certain time at the audition location. This was great because there were literally thousands of people waiting in line, but I knew that my time on television was assured!

Then, wearing my belly dancing costume and having my haircut, as usual, so that I had a baldhead, I got the call from the reporter. I cut ahead of thousands of people who had waited in line for hours to get to the front of the line where my reporter awaited me.

During my interview, I was energetic, entertaining and I even taught the reporter a few belly dancing moves. It was fabulous! What I did next was the best *Schmingling* tip. After the interview aired, I asked all of my friends and family to email or call in to the television station that covered the interview.

Even though only ten members of my family emailed, it was enough to make that reporter very happy! In her entire career, she had never received such a great response to a story. The reporter's supervisor didn't even notice that everyone who emailed had the same last name.

After that interview, I wanted more airtime. I had to find a way to get back on the news. I re-read the bio of the reporter and saw that she loved to skydive. I emailed her and invited her to go skydiving with me, and, by the way, I told her to feel free to bring her camera crew. The reporter agreed to my skydiving invitation, and we had a blast. She didn't bring the television station's camera crew, but I hired the camera crew of the skydiving company to record the reporter saying some pretty wonderful things about me! Unfortunately that reporter relocated to another state, but I realized that the tips I got from Paula Froelich really worked.

Schmingling
Photo Gallery

with

FAITH McKINNEY

Renowned economist and writer
Dr. Julianne Malveaux

Faith with Indiana Governor Mike Pence

Faith with world renowned motivational speaker Les Brown

Faith and ICIndymag.com editor Harrison Page
after interview with
legendary newsman Dan Rather

Faith with legendary Jazz musician
George Benson

Faith with actor, activist and author Hill Harper

Faith with Civil Rights Leader Julian Bond

Faith interviewing gospel artist Kirk Franklin

Faith with journalist Soledad O'Brien

Faith with political commentator Tavis Smiley

Chapter 10

Pretend that Everyone Loves You

As an introvert and a very shy person, I had a hard time making a great first impression when entering a room. I knew that if I wanted to be perceived as a star, I needed to move like stars move in order to feel like stars feel. If you've ever seen the movie *Legally Blond,* you'll recall the scene when the slightly out of place Elle Woods and her dog, Bruiser Woods, first arrived at *Harvard*, driving her *Porsche*, followed by a huge moving truck with all her pretty pink belongings. Elle pours Bruiser a bowl of water and reminds him, "*It's okay. Everyone will love you.*"

I mention this because this is the message I tell myself every time I enter a room. I've found that I do need to remind myself that it is truly up to me the way I am received.

As mentioned before, Oprah says:

> *"You are responsible for the energy you bring to a room."*

This means, whether you are happy or sad, that the energy you carry is felt by everyone in the room as soon as you step in! Often, the energy you project is reflected right back at you.

The way you carry your body has a lot to do with your feelings and your attitude. Body language also communicates more about you than you reveal verbally.

The section below is what I discovered about body language from a website by author David Straker, *www.Changingminds.org*.

> Body language is: The unconscious messages your posture conveys to observers. Suppose you are attending an event where every aspect of the occasion is just right. The venue is comfortably appointed, and the attendees seem to be from various backgrounds and various educational levels, making for an interesting mix. The energy in the room appears to be good. Everything externally appears to be perfect.
>
> Notice the type of people you are attracted to. By attractive, in this case, I don't mean sexually attractive, necessarily. Your goal will be to ask yourself why they seem to catch your eye in a positive way. Do they seem to have the attention of many people? How are they dressed? Is it appropriate for the venue and occasion? What is their body language saying about them?
>
> How do you interpret body language and what does your body language say to others? Here's a short translation about the underlying meaning of some overt body language.
>
> - Smile showing teeth – means you are open and friendly.
> - Smile not showing teeth – means, possibly, that you may be insincere in your greeting of others. You may not be happy in your current situation.
> - Crossed arms - means that you are defensive about something. Crossing arms in front of your chest or stomach area is often used unconsciously as a protective gesture used to guard your soul or your heart from hurtful words or harmful intentions.
> - Arms uncrossed - means the person is receptive to you and your ideas.

Chapter 10 Pretend that Everybody Loves You

- Chin down covering throat area - could mean a person may not be completely confident in what he/she is saying.

- Chin up exposing throat area- says that the person is extremely confident about what he/she is saying. It also means that the person's thoughts and actions are congruent with his/her own internal beliefs.

- Standing with feet apart - is a power stance. This is often used by people unconsciously claiming their territory.

- Standing feet crossed - could mean the person is self-conscious about something.

- Eye contact - Eye contact is an entire language in itself. The saying that "the eyes are the windows to the soul" is true. The eyes are the most telling in regards to truth telling. Have you ever seen a game of poker on television where many of the players wear dark sunglasses hiding their eyes? That's because other top players understand that when a player is bluffing, the pupils of their eyes get smaller. Why? This is to hide the true intentions of the person. You cannot control this action. Your eyes will reveal the truth.

Because I believe that understanding the language of the eye is so important, I included some of the definitions from David Straker's website in the section above because reading body language is an essential aspect of networking. Many times the things that people are thinking but won't say are revealed through body language. It is important to understand whether you or your ideas are being accepted or rejected. Deciphering body language is required to decipher the truth.

My friend and mentor, Linda Clemons, is an expert at reading body language. She travels the world, speaking and training C-level sales professionals, attorneys and even *FBI* agents in the nuances of reading and interpreting body language. If you've never seen Linda read someone's body language, you are missing the most amazing and accurate body language reading in the world. She can even tell if you did the night before!

If you'd like more information, contact Linda at:
www.lindareadspeople@gmail.com.

Schmingling works when you are prepared. Understanding the language others are speaking with their bodies will give you a tremendous advantage because most people are not aware of what their own bodies are saying when their mouths are possibly saying something totally opposite.

Recently, my friend, personal trainer and business colleague, Alicia Clark, and I were talking over the phone about our futures. We are both passionate about the courses our lives are taking. Over the last two years, Alicia lost nearly 50 pounds, overcame extremely disheartening circumstances, and is now a fitness trainer, fit model and speaker.

Alicia is gorgeous - a natural beauty. However, in photos taken of Alicia on the runway during a fashion show, I noticed that her head was often down and her neck extended forward in what Supermodel Tyra Banks calls "The Monster Pose". It's a fairly menacing look for a model or anyone whose body uses this stance.

I advised Alicia to elongate her neck and stand straight. Elongating the neck opens up the throat area, exuding confidence, and allowing others to be receptive to you.

The next day I received a text from Alicia stating *"Good afternoon... Thank you in regards to yesterday...telling me to elongate my neck...it amazed me how I attracted new people in less than 24 hours... and they pointed out that particular body part."*

I'm extremely proud of Alicia; she now understands the importance of sending the correct message with your body. I'm sure she will pay attention from now on.

What do you want your audience to say about you? Now that you understand more about body language and eye language, you can now manage how others will see you and what they will say about you.

Chapter 10 Pretend that Everybody Loves You

I've always lived by the following axiom: *"If I'd be embarrassed for my mother or my husband to see me doing what I'm considering doing, then I won't do it."*

In this age of camera phones, video surveillance and hidden cameras, now, more than ever before, being aware of and controlling how others see you is critical! I can't stress this point enough! There are television shows whose entire premise is observing the body language of people who are in the midst of criminal activity. The actions of the subject are analyzed and scrutinized by an anonymous voice describing the intentions of the person to the audience. How does the voice know the intentions of this person? He's using *Body Language Interpretation*.

Have you ever gone to a restaurant and observed a couple at the next table arguing? Could you tell who the offender was in this case? Then you are an interpreter of body language. Everyone does it. It's a natural form of communication that often says more than mere words can express.

Chapter 11

Don't Break Character

Being authentic is a buzzword or phrase popularized by Oprah Winfrey on her long running television show, and now on her *OWN Network*. Being authentic means that your personality, actions, and beliefs are in complete agreement. In other words, you are aligned with your purpose. The words you speak mirror your actions and represent your beliefs. Being authentic also means you have integrity, and integrity is truth; it's being who you truly are all of the time.

Becoming authentic is a sure sign of personal maturation. My own personal journey to becoming authentic took many years and many different roads. Because of my many experiences, which included both battles and triumphs, I've learned that I will stand up to support certain causes even if it means losing my own life. It also means that I may no longer stand up for causes that no longer represent who I am and what I believe in.

This principle correlates in acting to "staying in character." Many great actors, like Denzel Washington and Robert DeNiro, are notorious for staying in character even when not on the movie set. In fact, they are known to remain in character during the entire rehearsal and filming process! In acting, this is quite a feat because the actor must first research his character extensively. This means that the actor must study history if it is a real person or he must study the literature or interview the author of the manuscript, if possible, in order to truly understand the character.

In the movie *Avatar, Academy Award* winning director, James Cameron, had to create an entire culture - from the spoken language to body movements, climate, gestures even sub-cultures - in order to create and make real his characters in this ground-breaking movie. Years of extensive research were done on the creation of a language alone. The movie production company took the cast to a Hawaiian island jungle in order to teach them how to walk and move about in the fictitious land created via computer. In the end, a complete awe-inspiring and believable new world was brought to the big screen and was received with rave reviews.

As a *Schmingling*, you live your history and experience every day. In order to become more authentic and true to your core values, you must analyze your beliefs and decide whether you would be willing to defend your beliefs even if it means you may suffer or go through some difficult circumstances in the process. You must also ask yourself if your actions match your words, your beliefs, and your character.

I love watching movies where an actor is portraying a person from another country, such as England or Ireland. I like to listen to hear the actor's true native accent come out as he speaks his lines. Many times, the difference is very subtle, such as the actor's pronunciation of the letter "r". Or if he's portraying a Japanese person, there will more than likely be many instances where the actor's native tongue will prevail.

Have you ever watched a movie about gladiators but noticed one of the medieval characters was wearing a watch?

I know these are very subtle faux pas, but often people determine a person's trustworthiness by extremely subtle and sometimes unconscious awareness of some inconsistencies the person has displayed. Many times people, when mulling over the character of a person, will say things like *"There's just something about him/her that I don't like,"* or, *"There's something about her that I love!"* or, *"She has the 'IT' Factor!"* These attributes are difficult to describe, but it is often the person's authenticity, or lack thereof, that makes the difference.

If the shoe fits, it shouldn't be a stretch.

In the pursuit of authenticity, there will be times you won't feel so "authentic." Feeling as if you are wearing a mask when you are searching for your authentic self is very common; this feeling occurs when you begin examin-

Chapter 11 **Don't Break Character**

ing yourself in order to determine your truth.

Classifying yourself often means putting yourself into a category with which you may not completely identify. This may not feel authentic because some aspects of this classification don't align with your experiences or your beliefs. This is an important step in becoming authentic because the incorporation of subtle qualities and values in your personality create your authentic self within a classification. This is also the beginning of creating your personal brand, which we spoke of in a previous chapter.

Authenticity - Fake it 'til you make it!

Authenticity, like the perfect shoe, should be a good fit, not a stretch!

Faking Confidence

> *"The most important thing is honesty: if you can fake that, you've got it made."*
>
> - George Burns

This quote from comedian George Burns is hilarious because it's so true! Many people have to seemingly fake confidence until it becomes second nature. Faking confidence isn't necessarily a bad thing. Study powerful, confident people, such as Oprah Winfrey and Tony Robbins; you will notice certain power stances they take when they want to feel in control of a situation. Motivational speaker, Tony Robbins, often takes his audience through a series of vigorous, heart pumping exercises that promote feelings of invigoration, power and assurance.

His routine often includes vigorous movement and *Emotional Feeling Techniques* that associate feelings with bodily movement, life force and energy. These movements put your mind and body in a state of confusion of sorts when the fast, ostensibly aggressive motion of your body allows your mind to go into a near "fight or flight" state. This mock aggression, along with the fact that there are thousands of people in the room doing the very same actions, mimics the actions of a very confident, assertive person.

I recall, as a very shy pre-teen, studying and imitating all the actions of my more popular classmates. I was painfully shy and extremely insecure, but I knew there was a gregarious, confident person lying just beneath the surface just screaming to come out.

My father was my hero. Even when I was a child, he encouraged me to read books on body language, imitate the good qualities of the people I admired, and listen to the flow of the popular kids' conversations. So I took note of their subtle gestures and stances. I consciously studied their body language for clues to their appeal.

As I did this, I gleaned helpful information that I incorporated into my new personality. One problem was that, while I was determined to change, my classmates didn't get that memo and continued to treat me as the same extremely shy girl they'd always known.

Fortunately, my freshman year of high school was the first year of desegregation in my school district. This meant that I was able to try out my new personality with an entirely new group of people who had neither a preconceived knowledge about me nor my past introverted behavior. While my transformation was not drastic, I did run for a seat on the Student Council, which I won! To date, that was by far my biggest leap into extroversion, and I continued to study the behavior of my more popular classmates.

Nearly thirty years later, my old high school classmates still remember me as very quiet and sweet. I know I have made a lot of progress as I gained confidence by joining clubs and interacting with other students. Now, I continue to study successful, powerful people on television. Oprah Winfrey is my favorite subject because her body movements and facial expressions are often unscripted. Oprah is indeed a powerhouse, and she carries herself that way. While being open and approachable, her body language exudes authority and assurance. Many times her insecurity is subtle but noticeable to the trained eye. Oprah is my standard of excellence. Because Oprah and I are of similar backgrounds, it is logical to me that her model of confidence, strength and influence are my gold standard.

Chapter 11   Don't Break Character

In my office, I have vision boards containing photographs of Oprah in more candid shots where she is more of her authentic self. As I go through my life, I imitate those photos of her when I find myself in situations like those I believe to be in those pictures. Now it seems that the word on the street is that I'm the next Oprah!

Learning your lines

"The whole essence of learning lines is to forget them so you can make them sound like you thought of them that instant."

- Glenda Jackson

Chapter 12

Understand the Jargon of Your Industry

Understanding the jargon of your industry is essential to *Schmingling* endeavour. If you are in a specific industry and you network at a convention for that specific industry, it is vitally important for you to understand the words, the phrases, and the nuances that the people in that industry use in order to communicate better and more efficiently.

Every industry has its own, specific vocabulary words that it uses. Some words are acronyms for other words, or acronyms for procedures. It's important, going into a networking event, to know the jargon that may be used in that particular event. This is necessary so that you can feel confident that you are prepared for your *Schmingling* event. You must understand the vocabulary that will be used, otherwise you'll be lost, and your lack of knowledge will stick out like a sore thumb.

How many times have you met someone new at an event; you go to speak to him and try to discern how knowledgeable he is about your particular industry. After only a few seconds of listening to this person speak, you know, without a doubt, that this person is out of place in your networking group because his industry vocabulary is limited.

How to Craft Your Elevator Speech

Because an elevator speech is so important, I am including this article written by David Meilach from *BusinessNewsDaily*, along with expert contributors, describing aspects of a good elevator speech. With just precious seconds to make an impression, nailing an "elevator pitch" can come down to what you do and don't say. However, striking the balance between deciding what to include and what to leave out presents an interesting and difficult dilemma for most people when delivering the brief summation of what his/her company is about. To help, *BusinessNewsDaily* spoke with business professionals to see what every elevator pitch must include. The following are excerpts from this article:

Hook them early

"Eighty percent of your success will depend on your opening line — aka the hook or the headline. The hook must snag your listener's interest and make them want to know more. Do this right and your prospects will follow you wanting more. A good story will deliver big results. The story demonstrates your product or service to the person you are talking to." – Bert Martinez, Founder and President of *Bert Martinez Communications*

Know your audience

"When crafting your elevator pitch, you first need to think about who you'll be in the elevator with. A good elevator pitch will shift depending on the audience you're trying to reach. Lead with the information that the recipient will care most about, and the rest will follow." – Andrew Cross, Account Director at *Walker Sands Communications*

Remember what you are trying to accomplish

"Remember you want to stand out and generate excitement. Don't regurgitate a memorized pitch that sounds like the last five seconds of a pharmaceutical ad. Personally, when I hear a pitch, I don't necessarily want to feel like I am being pitched to. I would rather have it be more conversational. One good technique is to start with the problem you are trying to solve, the way the current alternatives are

Chapter 12 Understand the Jargon of Your Industry

lacking, and then briefly describe your solution." – John Torrens, Assistant Professor of *Entrepreneurial Practice* at *Syracuse University's Whitman School of Management*

Create a relationship

"An elevator speech is an important networking tool. It should serve as a 'verbal' business card that provides a brief, compelling introduction to one's company and intrigues new acquaintances to seek more information. Your greatest strength while networking is to be a good listener. Readily share another fact or two about your business if you're asked questions following your elevator speech. Be sure to keep that next statement brief. Then, at your earliest opportunity, express an interest in your new acquaintance. Learn as much as you can about this individual without monopolizing his or her time. The information you gain will provide insight as you proceed with efforts to build a genuine, mutually beneficial relationship." — Juana Hart, founder of *J-Hart Communications*

Be passionate

"Most people include 'what' they do in their elevator pitch but they forget to include the 'why' they do it. I suggest including the 'why' as a way to show your passion. Finally, finish by asking the other person what they do because it starts an actual conversation and allows you to actually connect, even after the elevator ride is over." — Stacey Hawley, founder of *Credo*

Have value

"Besides telling people what your product or service is, you need to make sure to include information on the value of the product to the customer. It's not enough to explain to someone why they need it. You can't just say what something is — you have to go beyond because we live

in a world that's flooded with elevator pitches." — Kristen Fischer, author of *When Talent Isn't Enough: Business Basics for the Creatively Inclined* (Career Press 2013)

Don't forget your closing

"Your elevator pitch is simply an introduction to your company, not a sale you have to close. End by summarizing your main talking points and offering a way for the prospect to get in touch with you. So, be sure to have your business card on hand." — Alex Membrillo, founder and CEO of *Cardinal Web Solutions*

The above topics were key inputs that I felt would add as much value for you as they did for me.

How to Speak the Language of Schmingling

The language of *Schmingling* is to be spoken only with cool, collected confidence, which can be challenging. The challenge does not come from the words that are spoken. The challenge lies in believing the words that are spoken.

Schmingling requires a measure of confidence in the way you describe yourself and your niche, or in other words, what is unique to you.

Blatant *Schmingling* requires the use of the phrase: "*I am the world's foremost authority on...*" or, "*I am a leading expert in the field of...*"

The phrase I use is: "*I am the country's foremost authority on self-promotion strategy.*"

I know this may sound a bit intimidating to say, but I can back it up, and I'll show you how.

Chapter 13

Don't Be a Schmuck - Look the Part

"First impressions are lasting impressions"

Your wardrobe and your outer appearance say a lot about who you are on the inside, and although we were taught not to judge people by their cover, your outer appearance speaks volumes. And, truthfully, you are judged by your outer appearance before anything else. Therefore your wardrobe must be impeccable and your grooming habits should be likewise.

The saying, "*First impressions are lasting impressions*" should be the mantra for all *Schminglers*. Are you happy with the way you look? Does your outer appearance say to the world what you intend for it to say? Does your outer appearance represent your gifts and talents? Your appearance should make it easier for the influencer, with whom you are trying to connect, to want to connect with you.

When you tell people what you do for a living, do they appear to be shocked or surprised? If so, maybe your appearance doesn't match what it is that you do or what it is that you like doing.

If you are a CEO of a *Fortune 500 Company* who sports tattoos and likes to ride his Harley motorcycle to work, there may be a bit of a disconnect between your appearance and your position, depending on the company. You may be able to hide those tattoos on your arm, but also know that they are definitely a no-no in the boardroom.

Are you a nurse who enjoys the look and feel of body piercings? You may want to reevaluate your priorities. Many patients prefer nurses and medical professionals without piercings and tattoos.

Take a look in the mirror. Do you like what you see? Aside from maybe the 10 or 15 or 50 pounds you might want to lose, notice how you appear to others. Ask yourself these questions as you face yourself in front of a full-length mirror:

- Looking at yourself, are your clothes fitting properly?
- Are your sleeves too long?
- Would your pants be perfect if they were tailored?
- Are your pants too short or too tight?
- Does the color you are wearing flatter your skin tone?
- Are the clothes that you're wearing faded and well-worn?
- Are there holes or stains? If so, get rid of these items immediately!

People do notice stains and holes and unflattering fit. What you wear says so much about you as a person, so much so that you could possibly be denied an interview by a potential employer because of your appearance. Don't let this happen to you! If you lack confidence in shopping for clothes, there are several department and specialty stores that you can go to that will help you find suitable outfits appropriate for your industry. Macy's has a free personal shopping service that provides knowledgeable and style-conscious personnel that can help you find the right fit for your body.

Understand that many clothes will not fit right off the rack. To ensure a perfect fit, consult with a skilled tailor who can sculpt your clothes to fit the body that you have right now. I find that *Macy's* has a wide variety of affordable, quality clothing with styles that suit many body types. If you're like me, your body is not proportional in size. My top is smaller than my bottom, so sometimes it's easier for me to go to a store that specializes in clothes that are made to fit my body shape, because, in the end, I always look so much better because I didn't try to squeeze into something that wasn't meant for my body.

Chapter 13   Don't Be a Schmuck – Look the Part

Another great way to know if you are dressing appropriately for your industry is to notice how the leaders in your industry dress. Check out their pictures on *LinkedIn* or *Google*, and their websites. Notice what they are wearing. Pay attention to the colors they've chosen to wear. Are they dressed predominantly in black or navy blue or gray? If so, you may want to consider those colors as your main staple. Always follow the lead of the leader in matters such as this.

Are you afraid to lose your own personality while trying to conform to business dress? You can always use accessories to add a bit of your own personality to any outfit. Make sure it's not distracting, but merely reflects a little of who you are without being offensive.

When I meet people that I don't know, and they tell me their stories, which include the fact that they are successful or they hold a leadership position, I do judge them by their clothing. I notice the quality of the person's shoes and tie. I evaluate the saturation of the colors in the garments they are wearing. Many times, successful people will dress the part. It's really just that simple.

If what you're wearing doesn't match who you say you are, it will show. Any discerning person will be able to tell. Of course there are a few exceptions to this theory. There are some people who, despite their higher status in business, choose not to conform or dress the part. Some of the exceptions are power hitters like Bill Gates and the late Steve Jobs. When you are *Schmingling*, it's important to look the part of the position that you want.

When I worked at the *Post Office* as a janitor, I worked there in that position for over fifteen years, but I knew that every time I stepped out of the *Post Office*, I was considered a celebrity because of my large fan base and many online celebrity interviews. For that reason, I could not be seen in a janitor's uniform.

I starred in the web soap opera, *Confessions* (*www.Confessions55.com*), and I was the host of a very popular networking organization, Successful Thinkers of Indianapolis, as well as, I was working on my speaking career. Yes, I was embarrassed by my job, though not ashamed of it, because it was good honest work, and working as a janitor paid the bills. When I went to work as a janitor, I made sure to dress as if I were going to a luncheon with friends. This meant that many times I dressed better than my *Postmaster* did. I never wanted to be seen as just the janitor, because I knew that wasn't who I was. In fact there were many times when, because I held a broom or a dustpan in my hand, the customers were confused because they thought I had a position of higher authority. They would ask: "*Wow, why are you out here sweeping the parking lot, or why are you out here shoveling the snow?*" I would always reply, "*We all need to help out.*"

Many days dressing my best helped me feel my best. Most days I wouldn't feel like cutting the grass, cleaning toilets or mopping floors - all jobs that needed to be done on a regular basis. There were also a great many times that I would do my work while wearing a beautiful silk blouse and pearls. Dressing for success helped me endure through many days when I felt like quitting.

Make up; Take it Easy!

Ladies, makeup is an important part of your grooming and beauty routine. I consider a woman's eyes to be a major aspect of a woman's beauty. I know many women do not want to arch their eyebrows (including my own mother), but arched eyebrows frame the face and draw attention to the eyes. Facial hair is not pretty on most women; so, if a visit to your trusted stylist is in order, please make an appointment right away.

Face Off

For many years I suffered with terrible acne up until my late 30's. My acne devastated and traumatized me so much that I could not look people in the eye. My self-esteem was at rock bottom for most of my life.

When I found an affordable treatment for my acne, I gained the confidence I needed to begin living the life I'd always wanted. My self-esteem rose and has remained very high even when my face unexpectedly broke out in acne again. Apparently, when you're in your mid-40s, hormones wreak havoc on some women's face, so I am now experiencing a second bout with adult

Chapter 13 Don't Be a Schmuck – Look the Part

acne. At this writing my face looks like a game of connect-the-dots. My skin looks nothing like the beautiful, smooth, brown skin I had just a few months ago. And although my self-esteem is high now, it doesn't diminish the devastating effects acne has on my ego.

I've noticed that when I walked throughout the mall without makeup, exposing my acne scars, I didn't want to look people in the eye. I wanted to be invisible.

Thank goodness there was a knowledgeable and empathetic sales clerk at a product kiosk where I purchased my cosmetics and skin care products. She suggested products to conceal my dark marks so that my skin looks smooth and even. No one would ever know what was underneath until I wiped my makeup off. Now my skin appears flawless and with minimum eye shadow and lip gloss, my face looks natural and very approachable. I feel like myself again!

Chapter 14

Gifts that Keep On Giving - Offering Access

Do you have access to a game or backstage passes to a sold out show, or do you personally know someone that the person you are trying to attract may want to meet? You can leverage access in this way. Access may include being led back stage to shake the hand of a respected author, or it may be VIP seating that you get for free. Whatever it is, make it a gesture of goodwill that you offer your influencer and not a gesture of desperation.

Gift's They'll Never Forget

Another way to make someone feel special is by offering them a token gift. Once I had the great opportunity to interview gospel singer, composer, and author, Kirk Franklin. I wanted to give him a gift to say thank you for the interview. I wanted the gift to be something that showed thoughtfulness, yet be something that I could afford. As I did my research on Kirk Franklin, I noticed in more than one of his video blogs that he was eating a bag of almonds. He was eating so ferociously that I could barely understand what he was saying.

I thought to myself, "*This would be a great thank you gift for the interview.*" So I researched the bag of almonds that he was eating, and I found his brand at a local grocery store where I found out those almonds were not cheap! Each bag cost nearly nine dollars, but I decided to get two bags, just in case.

Before the interview, I handed Mr. Franklin a bag of almonds saying, "*Here, Mr. Franklin. I got these for you.*" He replied, "*Thank you. These are my favorites.*" I responded to Mr. Franklin with pride and confidence, "*I know. I did my research!*"

We sat down to do the interview, and as Mr. Franklin was running a little late for the lecture he was there to give, he ran into the Green Room leaving his bag of almonds behind. I noticed his almonds sitting there on the floor next to the chair where he left them. I was determined that he was going to get those almonds. Not thinking, I yelled, "*Hey Mr. Franklin, don't forget your nuts!*" That was embarrassing, to say the least, but Kirk Franklin had a great sense of humor, and I don't believe he'll forget that for a long, long time.

Make Them Feel Special

Everyone wants to feel special, especially people who are used to getting special treatment. Nothing makes people feel more special than spending time around a table full of good friends and good food. There's a reason why mealtimes have always been where deals are made. There is something intrinsically natural about eating delicious food and bonding. I can't explain it, but there is something to it.

After you've made that initial connection with your influencer, invite them to dinner or lunch. Who knows? It may be the beginning of a beautiful friendship.

And The Award Goes To...

In order to gain access to hard-to-get influencers who may not ordinarily attend your event, this tactic works very well. Honor your influencer with an elaborate awards ceremony. No one wants to turn down an award, right?

I first used this tactic with great success with a gentleman who brings celebrities, thought leaders and political figures to Indianapolis to speak to

Chapter 14 Gifts that Keep On Giving - Offering Access

audiences who may not ordinarily have an opportunity to see them in person. My objective was to gain access to interview the celebrity speakers as well as exposing this very well-connected man to my group of *Successful Thinkers*, so we presented him with an award for his contributions to the community.

Not only did he bring his wife to the event, but he also brought about ten members of his family and friends to watch him receive his award. We took lots of pictures and shared them on *Facebook.* So now, not only do I have easier access to significant interviews with notable people, but I also have solidified a lasting relationship with a leader in my community.

Chapter 15

How to Prove You Are an Expert in Your Field

I wrote a book about self-promotion - you're reading it now! I've achieved my own success in self-promotion. I have photos, and I have many testimonials attesting to the fact. I'm definitely not advising you to lie, or even stretch the truth. I am advising you to toot your own horn, but only as much as you can back it up.

The easiest way to be an expert is to find the narrowest niche in your field of interest. For instance: if you want to be perceived as an expert in sports, you must first be extremely specific. Let's say the particular sport is auto racing. Inside racing you are interested in *Indy Car* open wheel racing. We'll become even more specific and focus on racing tires. Then we'll break it down to your knowledge of tires on certain wet asphalt surfaces. Then we'll go further to finally honing in on your expert knowledge of the matrix of the optimum composition of the racing tire to the wet surface of each specific racetrack in the *IRL*. Whew!

You must be THAT specific in your niche in order to define and defend your expert status. You'll also need physical proof in photos, articles you've written, articles written about you, and testimonials from credible sources in your industry. Documentation is vital to establishing yourself as an expert in your niche.

I admit, it took a long time for me to feel comfortable calling myself an expert and talking to people about my business and accomplishments, but doing so solidifies my position as an expert.

Chapter 16

Make Others Want to Connect With You

I knew that if I wanted to be seen as interesting and attractive to others, then I had to do interesting and attractive things. *Schmingling* is most effective if you are interesting and attractive. You need interesting things to discuss. You don't need to skydive or donate a kidney like I did, but you do need to have something interesting to talk about.

How do you become interesting? The easiest way to become interesting is to keep up with current events by reading periodicals like *The Wall Street Journal*, *The Economist*, and trade journals from your particular industry. Read books on a variety of topics in general but place emphasis on topics that you are interested in specifically.

The Internet is the perfect venue for learning about various subjects. Do interesting things! What interests you can be made interesting to others when you have personal experiences to share. Becoming interesting means celebrating the things you love and love to do.

If you are a collector, talk about your prized collection to others. Inform and educate them on the significance of your pieces.

If traveling is your thing, focus on and develop a story about a particularly interesting event that happened during your travels.

Why you need a story

Stories are an easy way to connect you to others on a more intimate level. Every successful person in any industry has a story. A story gives gravity, legitimacy and credibility to people, places or things.

If you are introverted like I am, you need to craft a story about yourself and about your interests in order to convey, verbally, the thoughts and ideas that are significant to you. Writing your story is a skill, which I am not qualified to teach. I would suggest finding an article written about individuals you admire and substitute facts from their story with facts from your own life. Read and re-read the results. Customize the story to suit the facts in your situation. Don't be intimidated by the adjectives the original authors use in their descriptions. Use them for your own story, and see how it works.

The important point to crafting your story is to believe the story as you re-tell it to others. You must believe that you are worthy of the complimentary words you say about yourself.

Chapter 17

Schmingling Won't Work if You Don't Have This

Schmingling will not work if you don't have courage.

Maya Angelou once said:

> *"Courage is the most important of all the virtues, because without courage you cannot practice any other virtue consistently."*

Telling complete strangers how wonderful and interesting and smart you are is very difficult. Our society teaches us to be humble and not boastful. Courage comes from practice and knowing that you are being authentic in everything you do.

I admit that *Schmingling* events can be very intimidating if you are not prepared. *Schmingling* means connecting through blatant self-promotion. Self-promotion means speaking highly about yourself in a confident and comprehensible manner.

You must rehearse your stories and be prepared to answer questions. If you are familiar with "elevator speeches", they often answer the questions of who, what, why, when and how in describing yourself. However, elevator speeches generally don't answer these questions: "*What do you need, or, how can I help you, specifically?*"

As a start-up business owner, you may be hesitant to divulge your weaknesses to others whom you perceive to be your influencers. I implore you to get over yourself for the good of your dream! You must know specifically who you are and what you need in order to connect you to where you need to be.

Whenever movie stars are on the Red Carpet these days, it seems the question is always, "*Who are you wearing?*" referring to the designer of the beautiful gowns or tuxes.

Designers often donate their very expensive haute couture gowns to the stars to wear and be seen in them on the *Red Carpet* in exchange for just a mention of their names on worldwide television. The celebs wearing the costly frocks know how important it is to answer the questions about the clothes and each piece of jewelry they are wearing in order to credit the individual designers.

Just as movie stars need to be able to answer these questions, you'll need to know the answers to some very predictable questions of your own. It may seem obvious, but questions like, "*What do you do?*" or "*How long have you been in business?*" may be questions that trip you up in a *Schmingling* situation.

I recall a young acquaintance of mine had recently started his a multilevel marketing business. It was apparent that he had attended quite a few of his company's rallies. He was enthusiastic about his business and eager to share the financial compensation plan with me. However, he didn't quite understand how to sell himself with the product. When I asked him what his business does, he replied, "*We do everything!*" Perplexed I asked, "*What do you sell?*" He replied, "*We sell everything.*"

It was clear to me that this young man could not field the questions posed to him. Because he was so eager to sell me on the product, he neglected to find out what I might need to make my life easier. And because he said his business has and does everything, and had no specific niche or expertise, I could not trust that he could deliver on his promises. He had no clue about how to answer questions about his new venture.

I've also been guilty of this faux pas. Before I figured out my niche of *Self-Promotion Through Blatant PR*, I couldn't explain what I did with any clarity. I was confused about how to best answer the question regarding what

Chapter 17 Schmingling Won't Work if You Don't Have This

I did for a living. At that time, I didn't want too many people to know that I worked for the *Postal Service* for nearly 25 years because I was embarrassed by the fact that I worked as a janitor for so many years. I knew I wouldn't be employed there much longer, but guilt and shame consumed me.

It took a while, but as my networking organization *Successful Thinkers of Indianapolis*, grew in popularity, the less I needed to answer those embarrassing questions. Many times my reputation preceded me, and members of my fan base would answer the questions for me. They would actually describe my business in ways that I never could.

Practice reciting your answers to predictable questions. This will give you the confidence to speak with clarity and authority because you'll know the answers.

Chapter 18

The Schmingler's Way to Enter a Room

Step and Repeat: The action of having someone step onto the Red Carpet, pose for the photographers, and leave. Just as the movie stars do on Awards night, *Schminglers* enter a room the same way: you smile into each camera (or in this case, look each person in the eye, quickly), strike a slight pose, lift your head up, pull your stomach in, etc.

This may be a new approach to you, but this is exactly the way you should enter each and every *Schmingling* event. It is important that you feel that you are the star of each *Schmingling* event you attend! This may take some getting used to, but I want you to consider for a moment that when you attend a *Schmingling* event, you want people to notice you. You want to give the best impression possible, just like movie stars do. This may take some practice, but trust me, it's well worth the effort.

Prior to your *Schmingling* events, stand straight and tall in front of a full-length mirror. Practice smiling a natural smile, hold your head up, stick your chest out, and suck your stomach in.

The first impression the people have of you should be that of confidence and energy. No one wants to connect with a sad, pitiful person, so make your entrance matter!

A game I play whenever I attend an event is pretending that I am walking the *Red Carpet*. I walk into the room close to the center of the room or to the nearest opening of space on the floor. I stop, strike a confident pose, smile, and look around for a friendly face. If I see one, I proceed to go and greet that person.

My BFF, Faith James, witnessed my little game. She commented on how everyone was noticing me and wondering who I was. The entire "Step and Repeat" process should last no longer than 20 seconds.

Try the "Step and Repeat" entrance. It really works!

Chapter 19

7 Rules for Schmingling Engagement

When you're attending a *Schmingling* event, always act as if all eyes are on you.

Although what you're attending is not a *Hollywood* movie premiere, it is your premiere, and you should be prepared. Here are some tips for gaining composure and confidence prior to a networking event:

1. Eat light and check your breath! Don't go to the event hungry but don't eat a heavy meal either. A good salad and some fruit and water should suffice before attending any event. Don't eat foods that don't agree with you. If you are lactose intolerant, please enjoy your garlic and ice cream after you *Schmingle*. You'll be doing us all a big favor!

2. Make sure your clothes and shoes are fit well and are comfortable and smell fresh. There's nothing worse than wearing smelly clothes and shoes that neither fit well nor look flattering on you when you're trying to make a good impression.

3. Travel light. Don't carry everything but the kitchen sink with you as you *Schmingle*. You should be unencumbered as you meet people. Always have one hand free for shaking.

4. Always have plenty of clean, fresh, current business cards on hand. It's embarrassing to make a connection and realize that you are not well prepared. Always carry business cards!

5. If you do not already have one, invest in a small, digital camera and take it with you to each *Schmingling* event so that you are prepared to take a photo of yourself and your influencer.

6. Also, carry a small, pocket notebook with you to record your influencer's contact information, in case he/she does not have a business card to give to you.

7. Finally, follow up by sending the influencer a note or card through *Send Out Cards*, and include a copy of the photo you took together in the correspondence. Trust me. This will make a lasting, positive impression!

Chapter 20

My Guaranteed, No Fail, Best Schmingling Tactic You Must Do Today!!!

I mentioned in several times in previous chapters that you need photographs for proof and credibility of you expert status. I can't tell you how valuable a great photograph is, especially when it includes you with a person of influence.

During election season, politicians hold private, fund-raising dinners for their supporters and campaign donors, as well as others who want to be associated with them. Often, attendees are charged anywhere from $1000.00 to $10,000 per plate, or more, just for the opportunity to have their pictures taken with the person of influence.

Being able to show the world that you associate with "movers and shakers" is relatively easy if you are prepared. But how do you influence the influencer? How do you set yourself apart from everyone when it comes to creating a lasting impression?

Send Out Cards!

According to *E-zine* articles, *Send Out Cards* is an online greeting card company. They have over 15,000 greeting cards in their catalogue, and almost 550 categories of different cards. *Send Out Cards* differs from an *eCard* service, where the cards are distributed to recipients electronically, because this service provides good old fashioned paper cards.

The sender of the card will choose a card from the catalog and then can edit it by adding a personal photo, a decorative border, clipart or other graphic element. The sender can then add a personal message to the card. Once the card is completed, *SOC* will print the card, stuff it, stamp it and mail it. A thoughtful greeting card is on its way to the recipient. The sender didn't have to wait in line at the store or go to the *Post Office*.

I always send a photo of my influencer and me and include a note inside thanking him/her and reminding them about the circumstance or event where the photo was taken. It's human nature to keep cards and photos of yourself and post them in a prominent place in your home or office. Influencers are no different. By posting these cards in a prominent place, the cards are seen by many more people in the influencer's life who will inevitably ask who the other person is in the photo. This triggers the influencer's memory of you yet again.

I use *Send Out Cards* to send personal invites and thank you cards to attendees of my *Schmingling* events. It's always a great touch.

Try *Send Out Cards* for yourself for FREE! I'm so convinced that you will be blown away by the results from using *Send Out Cards* that I've included three free cards for you to send to your influencer right now!

Go to: www.Sendoutcards.com/51782.

There you will find easy instructions describing how to use Send Out Cards.

Frequently Asked Schmingling Questions

I'm including FAQs here because *Schmingling* is such a radical departure from the way we were taught to network that I felt it was important to address my readers' queries.

Angela Felix asks: "*As a national performing/recording artist and actress, I need to meet a lot of people in order to keep working steadily. How do I parlay meetings into potential bookings without seeming desperate or arrogant?*"

> **Answer**: Playwright, actor, and producer, Stanley Bennett Clay, once told me the reason it seems the same actors get all the roles is because the Hollywood execs, producers and directors are very lazy. He states that the industry doesn't want to take the time to investigate or invest in new or undiscovered talent. My suggestion to you would be to stay in contact with these influencers you are meeting via *Send Out Cards*. By sending a card with a photo of you and your influencer together, you will be remembered. Send a card to them every other month, or whenever you have achieved a success in your career.
>
> Send pictures of you with other movers and shakers in your industry, as well. Doing this shows that you have connections. Also, don't be afraid to promote yourself, and don't be afraid to ask for the roles you want. Remaining uppermost in the minds of influencers will get you the roles you want and deserve.

Shante Marie Nicole asks: "*As a janitor, did you ever dream of seeing yourself in the position that you are in now, and did you appreciate the job as a janitor, or did you want to excel?*"

> **Answer**: This is a great question, Shante. The truth is that I always knew I would be in the position I am in today. I visualized it from the time I

was very young. I applied for the position of Clerk at the *Post Office* in 1987, fully intending on only working there until I finished college. Later that year, I was married and had my daughter. I also had a mortgage, car payments and bills. I needed to work, and the *Post Office* was, and still is, a source of a decent income, so I stayed there. I hired in as a Clerk working every weekend and nights. In 1995, I changed crafts in order to qualify to work during normal day hours and have weekends off. Because of my great schedule, time flexibility and close proximity to my daughter's care facility, I remained a janitor for many years.

T. Tanner-Starks asks: "What are the five top *Schmingling* tips?"

Answer: Thanks, Tanner. I mentioned "7 Rules..." earlier in this book, but for you, I will list ways I connected with several celebrities through *Schmingling*:

1. As an on-air personality (even though I had no prior experience) I interviewed my first *Hollywood* actor, Hill Harper, through *Steward and Associates Speaker* series. I support the series by purchasing a season ticket.

2. While serving as chauffer for my speaking coach, David Bridgeforth, I picked up motivational speaker, Les Brown and Oprah's makeup artist, Reggie Wells, in my "Mom Van".

3. I hijacked a picture with soulful singer, Howard Hewett, while he was still onstage singing at a church banquet.

4. In order to get interviews that others don't get, I contacted *Butler University*, whose *Diversity Lecture Series* often brings in top speakers who are open to interviews before their lectures. I've interviewed Kirk Franklin and Dan Rather through *Butler University*.

5. I chased down civil rights leader, Julian Bond, at the *Indianapolis International Airport* just for a photo! It was well worth the effort. (That's seven celebs!)

Frequently Asked Schmingling Questions

Keoini Wells says: *"Good luck and congrats on the book! Here's a question: How do you Schmingling if you're introverted or you have no charisma?"*

> **Answer:** Fantastic question! I love this one because I consider myself very introverted, but I had the desire to be an extrovert. I wrote this book for my introverted sisters and brothers who want to break out of their shells, but don't know how. *Schmingling* gives introverts permission to do things that they have always been taught not to do. This book is intended to give practical and practically free ideas to make you well-connected. The use of *Send Out Cards* is the perfect answer to this question.
>
> You don't need to speak to your influencer at all, and yet you make a lasting impression through pictures and/or thoughtful words on a greeting card. *Send Out Cards* is the perfect *Schmingling* tool!

Eric Zeedyk asks: *"I just moved to a new city and know next to no one... What would you recommend for me to meet and interact with some important contacts within my new community?"*

> **Answer:** Thanks Eric! Each community has nuances and flavors all their own.
>
> *Meetup.com* is a fantastic way to meet people who share your interests. It doesn't matter if you are into *Law of Attraction* or your pet pug. *Meetup.com* is a great way to create your very own community within your new community. *LinkedIn* is another way to build your business contacts, just remember that face-to-face interaction is the secret ingredient to building strong relationships.
>
> Another way to meet great people in your community is to find and attend a *SuccessfulThinkers* networking event in your new community. If there is none, you may consider starting your own and advertising it on sites like *Facebook* and *Meetup.com*. Hope this helps Eric.

Finally, I believe that our purpose here on Earth is to use all of our God-given gifts and talents to live the lives we desire, and to favorably impact the lives of others. The *Bible* says that our gifts will make room for us; but do you know what or who is the biggest impediment to your reaching your goals and dreams by using your gifts? YOU ARE! So my wish for you is that you take the courageous step of channeling those gifts, talents and skills to achieve your desires.

Yes, it takes courage, because first and foremost, you have to boldly declare your gifts through *Blatant Self-Promotion*! It works for me, and I guarantee you, it will work for you. I've shown you the way. Now, let me hear from you as you achieve one victory after another, and I'll share your stories with your fellow *Schminglers*!

Frequently Asked Schmingling Questions

Here is my contact information:

- Phone: (317) 626-0316
- Email: schmingling@gmail.com
- LinkedIn: Faith McKinney
- Twitter: @Faithmckinney
- Facebook: My personal page - Faith Moore-McKinney
- Facebook: My fan page - Faith McKinney - The Great Connector
- Websites: faithmckinney.com
  Schmingling.biz
  ICIndymag.com

Looking forward to celebrating your success!

FAITH McKINNEY

About the Author

FAITH McKINNEY

...known as "THE GREAT **CONNECTOR**," is the author of the book, *Schmingling - The Art of Being Well-Connected Through Blatant Self-Promotion*, and is an expert, focusing on *Schmingling* and relationship and credibility buildting, as well as, speaking on several topics pertaining to leveraging radical public relations to take you literally "from the janitor's closet to the corner office," or anywhere you want to go. Faith's message is geared toward fledgling and startup entrepreneurs, as well as, introverts looking to increase and strengthen their networks of social media and business and personal contacts, resulting in increased visibility and credibility.

Faith's passion is teaching others how to build their own industry platforms and how to establish their own, solid, loyal fan bases.

Overcoming her own, sometimes debilitating, shyness, Faith has served as Host and Lead Ambassador of *Successful Thinkers of Indianapolis* since 2010. *Successful Thinkers of Indianapolis* is a free, monthly networking and relationship building organization, which emphasizes a more personal approach to networking. By effectively utilizing social media, Faith has solidified her industry credibility while taking *Successful Thinkers of Indianapolis'* membership from 35 members to over 800 members within a mere two years.

Faith's success with *SuccessfulThinkers of Indianapolis* has led to a partnership with *ITT Technical Institutes* campuses in Indianapolis, where her networking and relationship building teaching has been added to their Business curricula. As well, Faith is on track to expand and partner with colleges and universities all over the country. She teaches networking etiquette, credibility formulas and radical public relations to students and to small and startup business owners.

Faith serves as on-air personality, photographer, and celebrity interviewer for *ICIndymag.com*, an online community magazine, where she covers local events and has conducted interviews with such celebrities as legendary TV journalists, Dan Rather and Soledad O'Brien, talk show host, author, political commentator and entrepreneur, Tavis Smiley, actor/activist, Hill Harper, military veteran and *Dancing With the Stars* winner, J.R. Martinez, and musical geniuses, Kirk Franklin and George Benson, just to name a few.

Faith has contributed to several books on topics including: *Laws of Attraction*, *Parenting Special Needs Children*, and *Relationships and Radical Public Relations*. She has also been quoted in the popular blog Loop 21. In addition, Faith has been mentioned in *Ebony Magazine*, and had a published interview in *The Wall Street Journal*.

Having experienced life as an exchange student living in Japan, Faith understands and appreciates all people and their cultural differences. She encourages people of all backgrounds to connect with each other.

Faith's strong desire to make a difference in the world inspired her to become an organ donor in 2009, when she donated her kidney, improving the life of a relative.

Faith lives in Indianapolis, Indiana with Jimmy, her husband of ten years, and children, Camille, Donovan and Mauricia.

Team Schmingling Bios

Sharon Chinn, Editor

As owner of *You've Got Something To Say!* Manuscript Writing and Editing Service, Sharon Chinn partners with authors by ghost-writing their manuscripts, editing their manuscripts and providing consultative services to help authors navigate the process of building their platforms or fan bases, determining their optimal publishing options, i.e., self-publishing, traditional publishing company, e-book publishing, etc., and referring authors to other professionals to develop their brands and promote their publications.

Ms. Chinn can be contacted at *youvegotsomethingtosay@mail.com* for further information about her services.

Annie Gonzales, Interior Designer, Copy Editor, Project Manager

With over 30 years of professional experience Annie is the Art Director of *FHL International* and a *owner/graphic designer* of *FOR HIS GLORY Design Studio*. Annie consults with her clients to create designs that express the passion of their project and let the glory of God shine through! By imaginative, stunning and inspirational designs of book interiors and covers, DVD and CD packaging, and all promotional materials, she prepares your art for print so that you can begin to enjoy the fruits of your gifting.

Annie provides *copy-editing service* to optimize the accuracy and readability of your writings. Grammar and punctuation is her specialty!

And as *project manager*, Annie works as a liaison between the author, editor, interior and cover designers. She critiques your book elements to ensure that your book is produced with quality and facilitates the book design process to keep the project on timeline.

To view Annie's creative online design portfolio visit *forhisglorydesigns.org*. Annie is ready to make your dreams become a reality! You may contact her at *annie@forhisglorydesigns.org* or *annie@fhlinternational.org* to learn more about all the creative services that Annie offers.

Sylvia Wilson, Proofreader

Sylvia is the CEO of *SDW-Executive Virtual Assistance*. She is a corporate executive administrative assistant, with extensive experience at the highest executive level with over 20 years of success in the corporate realm having successfully supported managers and business partners at both *IBM* and *Eli Lilly*.

Her strengths are in organization and detail, verbal and written communication skills just to name a few of her honed skills. She exercises exceptional judgment and prides herself on being a well-organized dependable professional who goes above and beyond because she handles your business as if it were her own.

You can contact her at *sylviadwilson@gmail.com* and her professional profile can be found on both *LinkedIn-www.linkedin/com/in/sylviadwilson* and her website *sdw-executivevirtualassistant.webs.com*.

Mark Emmet Foster, Cover Designer

Mark Foster has been an artist or a designer, a writer and a problem-solver for five decades. With a Master of Fine and Applied Arts degree from *Rochester Institute of Technology*, he has taught on the faculties of a host of American universities in International corporate industrial design and American integrated marketing and advertising firms. Having also held communications design management positions in industries as varied as polymer manufacture and health care, he has been published as the Creative Director for the *New York State Senate Office of Majority Communications*.

Mark was also a specialist in corporate identity and branding, mass communications standards and social marketing campaigns for the states of Pennsylvania and New York. Having also established and run *Fostering Words+Images*, he continues to produce beautiful, impactful, appropriate, and memorable online printed and exhibit information today, including the cover design of this book.

Online samples of his work can be viewed and read on the following websites: *facebook.com/markemmetfosterdesign*, *issuu.com/MarkEmmetFoster* and *markemmetfoster.com*. Mark can be reached at *mfoster463@att.net*.